THIS JOURNAL BELONGS TO

_____

_____

_____

_____

_____

DEDICATION

This book is dedicated to all the ones that love collecting tickets!

You are my inspiration in producing books and I'm excited to help in the planning of your next ticket collecting event.

How To Use This Ticket Collecting Log Book:

This ultimate ticket collecting notebook is a perfect way to track and record all your concert going memories. This unique ticket collection journal is a great way to keep all of your keepsake information all in one place.

Each interior page includes prompts and space to record the following:

1. Date of Ticket Event - Write the date you attended the event.

2. Details of Ticket - Record the details you find written on the ticket. so as to be reminded later when reminiscing...

3. Purchased From - Construct your story about where you bought this ticket from...

4. Ticket - Space to attach the actual ticket or a photo of the ticket.

5. Notes, record your thoughts - Stay on task by making a note of any special memories from this event.

6. If you are new to collecting tickets or have been doing this for a while, this ticket collection journal is a must have! Can make an awesome gift for the ticket collector, and will be a keepsake memory forever. Convenient size of 8 x 10 inches, 110 pages, quality white paper, soft matte finish cover, paperback.

Have Fun!

TICKET COLLECTION

Date of Ticket Event:

Details of Ticket:

Purchased/Found From

History Behind Ticket

Ticket

NOTES

TICKET COLLECTION

Date of Ticket Event:

Details of Ticket:

Purchased/Found From

_____

_____

_____

_____

History Behind Ticket

_____

_____

_____

_____

Ticket

NOTES

_____

_____

_____

_____

TICKET COLLECTION

Date of Ticket Event:

Details of Ticket:

Purchased/Found From

_____

_____

_____

_____

_____

History Behind Ticket

_____

_____

_____

_____

_____

Ticket

NOTES

_____

_____

_____

_____

_____

TICKET COLLECTION Date of Ticket Event:

Details of Ticket:

Purchased/Found From

_____
_____
_____
_____
_____

History Behind Ticket

_____
_____
_____
_____
_____

Ticket

NOTES

_____
_____
_____
_____

TICKET COLLECTION Date of Ticket Event:

Details of Ticket:

Purchased/Found From

_____
_____
_____
_____
_____

History Behind Ticket

_____
_____
_____
_____
_____

Ticket

NOTES

_____
_____
_____
_____

TICKET COLLECTION
Date of Ticket Event:

Details of Ticket:

Purchased/Found From

_____
_____
_____
_____

History Behind Ticket

_____
_____
_____
_____

Ticket

NOTES

_____
_____
_____
_____

TICKET COLLECTION

Date of Ticket Event: [_____]

Details of Ticket: [_____]

Purchased/Found From

_____
_____
_____
_____
_____

History Behind Ticket

_____
_____
_____
_____
_____
_____

Ticket

NOTES

_____
_____
_____
_____
_____

TICKET COLLECTION

Date of Ticket Event: [ ]

Details of Ticket: [ ]

Purchased/Found From

_____
_____
_____
_____
_____

History Behind Ticket

_____
_____
_____
_____
_____

Ticket

NOTES

_____
_____
_____
_____

TICKET COLLECTION Date of Ticket Event:

Details of Ticket:

Purchased/Found From

_____
_____
_____
_____

History Behind Ticket

_____
_____
_____
_____
_____

Ticket

NOTES

_____
_____
_____
_____

TICKET COLLECTION Date of Ticket Event:

Details of Ticket:

Purchased/Found From

_____
_____
_____
_____
_____

History Behind Ticket

_____
_____
_____
_____
_____

Ticket

NOTES

_____
_____
_____
_____
_____

TICKET COLLECTION

Date of Ticket Event: [_____]

Details of Ticket: [_____]

Purchased/Found From

_____
_____
_____
_____

History Behind Ticket

_____
_____
_____
_____
_____

Ticket

NOTES

_____
_____
_____
_____

TICKET COLLECTION

Date of Ticket Event:

Details of Ticket:

Purchased/Found From

_____

_____

_____

_____

_____

History Behind Ticket

_____

_____

_____

_____

_____

Ticket

NOTES

_____

_____

_____

_____

_____

TICKET COLLECTION

Date of Ticket Event:

Details of Ticket:

Purchased/Found From

History Behind Ticket

Ticket

NOTES

TICKET COLLECTION

Date of Ticket Event:

Details of Ticket:

Purchased/Found From

_____
_____
_____
_____
_____

History Behind Ticket

_____
_____
_____
_____
_____

Ticket

NOTES

_____
_____
_____
_____

TICKET COLLECTION

Date of Ticket Event: _____

Details of Ticket: _____

Purchased/Found From

_____
_____
_____
_____
_____

History Behind Ticket

_____
_____
_____
_____
_____

Ticket

NOTES

_____
_____
_____
_____

TICKET COLLECTION
Date of Ticket Event: [ ]

Details of Ticket: [ ]

Purchased/Found From

_____
_____
_____
_____
_____

History Behind Ticket

_____
_____
_____
_____
_____

Ticket

NOTES

_____
_____
_____
_____
_____

TICKET COLLECTION

Date of Ticket Event:

Details of Ticket:

Purchased/Found From

History Behind Ticket

Ticket

NOTES

TICKET COLLECTION

Date of Ticket Event:

Details of Ticket:

Purchased/Found From

_____
_____
_____
_____
_____

History Behind Ticket

_____
_____
_____
_____
_____

Ticket

NOTES

_____
_____
_____
_____

TICKET COLLECTION Date of Ticket Event:

Details of Ticket:

Purchased/Found From

_____
_____
_____
_____
_____

History Behind Ticket

_____
_____
_____
_____
_____

Ticket

NOTES

_____
_____
_____
_____

TICKET COLLECTION

Date of Ticket Event:

Details of Ticket:

Purchased/Found From

_____

_____

_____

_____

_____

History Behind Ticket

_____

_____

_____

_____

_____

Ticket

NOTES

_____

_____

_____

_____

_____

TICKET COLLECTION

Date of Ticket Event: _____

Details of Ticket: _____

Purchased/Found From

_____
_____
_____
_____
_____

History Behind Ticket

_____
_____
_____
_____
_____

Ticket

NOTES

_____
_____
_____
_____

TICKET COLLECTION

Date of Ticket Event: _____

Details of Ticket: _____

Purchased/Found From

_____
_____
_____
_____
_____

History Behind Ticket

_____
_____
_____
_____
_____

Ticket

NOTES

_____
_____
_____
_____
_____

TICKET COLLECTION

Date of Ticket Event:

Details of Ticket:

Purchased/Found From

_____
_____
_____
_____
_____

History Behind Ticket

_____
_____
_____
_____
_____

Ticket

NOTES

_____
_____
_____
_____
_____

TICKET COLLECTION Date of Ticket Event:

Details of Ticket:

Purchased/Found From

_____

_____

_____

_____

History Behind Ticket

_____

_____

_____

_____

_____

Ticket

NOTES

_____

_____

_____

_____

_____

TICKET COLLECTION
Date of Ticket Event:

Details of Ticket:

Purchased/Found From

_____
_____
_____
_____

History Behind Ticket

_____
_____
_____
_____
_____

Ticket

NOTES

_____
_____
_____
_____
_____

TICKET COLLECTION

Date of Ticket Event:

Details of Ticket:

Purchased/Found From

History Behind Ticket

Ticket

NOTES

TICKET COLLECTION Date of Ticket Event:

Details of Ticket:

Purchased/Found From

History Behind Ticket

Ticket

NOTES

TICKET COLLECTION

Date of Ticket Event: _____

Details of Ticket: _____

Purchased/Found From

_____
_____
_____
_____
_____

History Behind Ticket

_____
_____
_____
_____
_____

Ticket

NOTES

_____
_____
_____
_____

TICKET COLLECTION

Date of Ticket Event:

Details of Ticket:

Purchased/Found From

_____
_____
_____
_____

History Behind Ticket

_____
_____
_____
_____
_____

Ticket

NOTES

_____
_____
_____
_____
_____

TICKET COLLECTION Date of Ticket Event:

Details of Ticket:

Purchased/Found From

_____

_____

_____

_____

_____

History Behind Ticket

_____

_____

_____

_____

_____

Ticket

NOTES

_____

_____

_____

_____

TICKET COLLECTION

Date of Ticket Event:

Details of Ticket:

Purchased/Found From

_____
_____
_____
_____
_____

History Behind Ticket

_____
_____
_____
_____
_____

Ticket

NOTES

_____
_____
_____
_____
_____

TICKET COLLECTION Date of Ticket Event:

Details of Ticket:

Purchased/Found From

_____
_____
_____
_____

History Behind Ticket

_____
_____
_____
_____

Ticket

NOTES

_____
_____
_____
_____

TICKET COLLECTION

Date of Ticket Event:

Details of Ticket:

Purchased/Found From

_____
_____
_____
_____
_____

History Behind Ticket

_____
_____
_____
_____
_____

Ticket

NOTES

_____
_____
_____
_____

TICKET COLLECTION

Date of Ticket Event: _____

Details of Ticket: _____

Purchased/Found From

_____

_____

_____

_____

_____

History Behind Ticket

_____

_____

_____

_____

_____

Ticket

NOTES

_____

_____

_____

_____

TICKET COLLECTION

Date of Ticket Event:

Details of Ticket:

Purchased/Found From

_____
_____
_____
_____

History Behind Ticket

_____
_____
_____
_____
_____

Ticket

NOTES

_____
_____
_____
_____

TICKET COLLECTION
Date of Ticket Event:

Details of Ticket:

Purchased/Found From

_____
_____
_____
_____

History Behind Ticket

_____
_____
_____
_____
_____

Ticket

NOTES

_____
_____
_____
_____

TICKET COLLECTION

Date of Ticket Event:

Details of Ticket:

Purchased/Found From

History Behind Ticket

Ticket

NOTES

TICKET COLLECTION

Date of Ticket Event: [ ]

Details of Ticket: [ ]

Purchased/Found From

_____
_____
_____
_____

History Behind Ticket

_____
_____
_____
_____
_____

Ticket

NOTES

_____
_____
_____
_____

TICKET COLLECTION Date of Ticket Event:

Details of Ticket:

Purchased/Found From

_____
_____
_____
_____
_____

History Behind Ticket

_____
_____
_____
_____
_____

Ticket

NOTES

_____
_____
_____
_____
_____

TICKET COLLECTION
Date of Ticket Event:

Details of Ticket:

Purchased/Found From

_____

_____

_____

_____

_____

History Behind Ticket

_____

_____

_____

_____

_____

Ticket

NOTES

_____

_____

_____

_____

_____

TICKET COLLECTION

Date of Ticket Event: [   ]

Details of Ticket: [   ]

Purchased/Found From

_____
_____
_____
_____

History Behind Ticket

_____
_____
_____
_____
_____

Ticket

NOTES

_____
_____
_____
_____

TICKET COLLECTION

Date of Ticket Event:

Details of Ticket:

Purchased/Found From

_____
_____
_____
_____
_____

History Behind Ticket

_____
_____
_____
_____
_____

Ticket

NOTES

_____
_____
_____
_____

TICKET COLLECTION

Date of Ticket Event:

Details of Ticket:

Purchased/Found From

_____
_____
_____
_____
_____

History Behind Ticket

_____
_____
_____
_____
_____

Ticket

NOTES

_____
_____
_____
_____
_____

TICKET COLLECTION Date of Ticket Event:

Details of Ticket:

Purchased/Found From

_____
_____
_____
_____
_____

History Behind Ticket

_____
_____
_____
_____
_____

Ticket

NOTES

_____
_____
_____
_____
_____

TICKET COLLECTION

Date of Ticket Event:

Details of Ticket:

Purchased/Found From

_____
_____
_____
_____

History Behind Ticket

_____
_____
_____
_____
_____

Ticket

NOTES

_____
_____
_____
_____
_____

TICKET COLLECTION

Date of Ticket Event:

Details of Ticket:

Purchased/Found From

_____
_____
_____
_____
_____

History Behind Ticket

_____
_____
_____
_____
_____

Ticket

NOTES

_____
_____
_____
_____
_____

TICKET COLLECTION

Date of Ticket Event:

Details of Ticket:

Purchased/Found From

History Behind Ticket

Ticket

NOTES

TICKET COLLECTION

Date of Ticket Event:

Details of Ticket:

Purchased/Found From

_____

_____

_____

_____

History Behind Ticket

_____

_____

_____

_____

_____

Ticket

NOTES

_____

_____

_____

_____

TICKET COLLECTION

Date of Ticket Event:

Details of Ticket:

Purchased/Found From

_____
_____
_____
_____

History Behind Ticket

_____
_____
_____
_____
_____

Ticket

NOTES

_____
_____
_____
_____
_____

TICKET COLLECTION

Date of Ticket Event: _____

Details of Ticket: _____

Purchased/Found From

_____
_____
_____
_____
_____

History Behind Ticket

_____
_____
_____
_____
_____

Ticket

NOTES

_____
_____
_____
_____
_____

TICKET COLLECTION Date of Ticket Event:

Details of Ticket:

Purchased/Found From

_____
_____
_____
_____
_____

History Behind Ticket

_____
_____
_____
_____
_____

Ticket

NOTES

_____
_____
_____
_____

TICKET COLLECTION

Date of Ticket Event:

Details of Ticket:

Purchased/Found From

_____
_____
_____
_____
_____

History Behind Ticket

_____
_____
_____
_____
_____

Ticket

NOTES

_____
_____
_____
_____

TICKET COLLECTION

Date of Ticket Event:

Details of Ticket:

Purchased/Found From

History Behind Ticket

Ticket

NOTES

TICKET COLLECTION

Date of Ticket Event:

Details of Ticket:

Purchased/Found From

_____
_____
_____
_____
_____

History Behind Ticket

_____
_____
_____
_____
_____

Ticket

NOTES

_____
_____
_____
_____
_____

TICKET COLLECTION Date of Ticket Event:

Details of Ticket:

Purchased/Found From

_____

_____

_____

_____

History Behind Ticket

_____

_____

_____

_____

Ticket

NOTES

_____

_____

_____

_____

TICKET COLLECTION

Date of Ticket Event: _____

Details of Ticket: _____

Purchased/Found From

_____

_____

_____

_____

_____

History Behind Ticket

_____

_____

_____

_____

_____

Ticket

NOTES

_____

_____

_____

_____

TICKET COLLECTION

Date of Ticket Event:

Details of Ticket:

Purchased/Found From

_____

_____

_____

_____

_____

History Behind Ticket

_____

_____

_____

_____

_____

Ticket

NOTES

_____

_____

_____

_____

TICKET COLLECTION
Date of Ticket Event:

Details of Ticket:

Purchased/Found From

_____
_____
_____
_____
_____

History Behind Ticket

_____
_____
_____
_____
_____

Ticket

NOTES

_____
_____
_____
_____

TICKET COLLECTION

Date of Ticket Event: [ ]

Details of Ticket: [ ]

Purchased/Found From

_____
_____
_____
_____
_____

History Behind Ticket

_____
_____
_____
_____
_____

Ticket

NOTES

_____
_____
_____
_____
_____

TICKET COLLECTION

Date of Ticket Event: [ ]

Details of Ticket: [ ]

Purchased/Found From

_____
_____
_____
_____
_____

History Behind Ticket

_____
_____
_____
_____
_____

Ticket

NOTES

_____
_____
_____
_____

TICKET COLLECTION

Date of Ticket Event: _____

Details of Ticket: _____

Purchased/Found From

_____

_____

_____

_____

_____

History Behind Ticket

_____

_____

_____

_____

_____

_____

Ticket

NOTES

_____

_____

_____

_____

_____

TICKET COLLECTION

Date of Ticket Event:

Details of Ticket:

Purchased/Found From

_____

_____

_____

_____

_____

History Behind Ticket

_____

_____

_____

_____

_____

Ticket

NOTES

_____

_____

_____

_____

TICKET COLLECTION

Date of Ticket Event: [   ]

Details of Ticket: [   ]

Purchased/Found From

_____
_____
_____
_____
_____

History Behind Ticket

_____
_____
_____
_____
_____

Ticket

NOTES

_____
_____
_____
_____
_____

TICKET COLLECTION

Date of Ticket Event: [____]

Details of Ticket: [____]

Purchased/Found From

_____

_____

_____

_____

History Behind Ticket

_____

_____

_____

_____

_____

Ticket

NOTES

_____

_____

_____

_____

TICKET COLLECTION

Date of Ticket Event:

Details of Ticket:

Purchased/Found From

_____

_____

_____

_____

History Behind Ticket

_____

_____

_____

_____

_____

Ticket

NOTES

_____

_____

_____

_____

TICKET COLLECTION

Date of Ticket Event:

Details of Ticket:

Purchased/Found From

_____

_____

_____

_____

_____

History Behind Ticket

_____

_____

_____

_____

_____

Ticket

NOTES

_____

_____

_____

_____

_____

TICKET COLLECTION

Date of Ticket Event: _____

Details of Ticket: _____

Purchased/Found From

_____
_____
_____
_____
_____

History Behind Ticket

_____
_____
_____
_____
_____

Ticket

NOTES

_____
_____
_____
_____
_____

TICKET COLLECTION

Date of Ticket Event:

Details of Ticket:

Purchased/Found From

History Behind Ticket

Ticket

NOTES

TICKET COLLECTION

Date of Ticket Event:

Details of Ticket:

Purchased/Found From

_____
_____
_____
_____
_____

History Behind Ticket

_____
_____
_____
_____
_____

Ticket

NOTES

_____
_____
_____
_____
_____

TICKET COLLECTION

Date of Ticket Event:

Details of Ticket:

Purchased/Found From

History Behind Ticket

Ticket

NOTES

TICKET COLLECTION

Date of Ticket Event:

Details of Ticket:

Purchased/Found From

_____
_____
_____
_____
_____

History Behind Ticket

_____
_____
_____
_____
_____

Ticket

NOTES

_____
_____
_____
_____

TICKET COLLECTION

Date of Ticket Event:

Details of Ticket:

Purchased/Found From

History Behind Ticket

Ticket

NOTES

TICKET COLLECTION

Date of Ticket Event:

Details of Ticket:

Purchased/Found From

_____
_____
_____
_____

History Behind Ticket

_____
_____
_____
_____
_____

Ticket

NOTES

_____
_____
_____
_____

TICKET COLLECTION Date of Ticket Event:

Details of Ticket:

Purchased/Found From

_____
_____
_____
_____
_____

History Behind Ticket

_____
_____
_____
_____
_____

Ticket

NOTES

_____
_____
_____
_____

TICKET COLLECTION
Date of Ticket Event:

Details of Ticket:

Purchased/Found From

_____
_____
_____
_____
_____

History Behind Ticket

_____
_____
_____
_____
_____

Ticket

NOTES

_____
_____
_____
_____

TICKET COLLECTION

Date of Ticket Event: [ ]

Details of Ticket: [ ]

Purchased/Found From

_____

_____

_____

_____

History Behind Ticket

_____

_____

_____

_____

Ticket

NOTES

_____

_____

_____

_____

TICKET COLLECTION

Date of Ticket Event:

Details of Ticket:

Purchased/Found From

_____
_____
_____
_____
_____

History Behind Ticket

_____
_____
_____
_____
_____

Ticket

NOTES

_____
_____
_____
_____
_____

TICKET COLLECTION

Date of Ticket Event: [   ]

Details of Ticket: [   ]

Purchased/Found From

_____
_____
_____
_____
_____

History Behind Ticket

_____
_____
_____
_____
_____

Ticket

NOTES

_____
_____
_____
_____

TICKET COLLECTION

Date of Ticket Event:

Details of Ticket:

Purchased/Found From

History Behind Ticket

Ticket

NOTES

TICKET COLLECTION

Date of Ticket Event:

Details of Ticket:

Purchased/Found From

_____

_____

_____

_____

History Behind Ticket

_____

_____

_____

_____

_____

Ticket

NOTES

_____

_____

_____

_____

TICKET COLLECTION
Date of Ticket Event:

Details of Ticket:

Purchased/Found From

_____
_____
_____
_____
_____

History Behind Ticket

_____
_____
_____
_____
_____

Ticket

NOTES

_____
_____
_____
_____
_____

TICKET COLLECTION Date of Ticket Event:

Details of Ticket:

Purchased/Found From

_____
_____
_____
_____
_____

History Behind Ticket

_____
_____
_____
_____
_____

Ticket

NOTES

_____
_____
_____
_____

TICKET COLLECTION

Date of Ticket Event:

Details of Ticket:

Purchased/Found From

_____

_____

_____

_____

_____

History Behind Ticket

_____

_____

_____

_____

_____

Ticket

NOTES

_____

_____

_____

_____

_____

TICKET COLLECTION

Date of Ticket Event:

Details of Ticket:

Purchased/Found From

_____
_____
_____
_____
_____

History Behind Ticket

_____
_____
_____
_____
_____

Ticket

NOTES

_____
_____
_____
_____

TICKET COLLECTION

Date of Ticket Event:

Details of Ticket:

Purchased/Found From

_____
_____
_____
_____
_____

History Behind Ticket

_____
_____
_____
_____
_____

Ticket

NOTES

_____
_____
_____
_____
_____

TICKET COLLECTION Date of Ticket Event:

Details of Ticket:

Purchased/Found From

_____
_____
_____
_____
_____

History Behind Ticket

_____
_____
_____
_____
_____

Ticket

NOTES

_____
_____
_____
_____
_____

TICKET COLLECTION

Date of Ticket Event: [ ]

Details of Ticket: [ ]

Purchased/Found From

_____
_____
_____
_____
_____

History Behind Ticket

_____
_____
_____
_____
_____

Ticket

NOTES

_____
_____
_____
_____
_____

TICKET COLLECTION

Date of Ticket Event:

Details of Ticket:

Purchased/Found From

History Behind Ticket

Ticket

NOTES

TICKET COLLECTION Date of Ticket Event:

Details of Ticket:

Purchased/Found From

_____
_____
_____
_____
_____

History Behind Ticket

_____
_____
_____
_____
_____

Ticket

NOTES

_____
_____
_____
_____

TICKET COLLECTION Date of Ticket Event:

Details of Ticket:

Purchased/Found From

_____
_____
_____
_____
_____

History Behind Ticket

_____
_____
_____
_____
_____

Ticket

NOTES

_____
_____
_____
_____

TICKET COLLECTION Date of Ticket Event:

Details of Ticket:

Purchased/Found From

_____
_____
_____
_____
_____

History Behind Ticket

_____
_____
_____
_____
_____

Ticket

NOTES

_____
_____
_____
_____
_____

TICKET COLLECTION
Date of Ticket Event:

Details of Ticket:

Purchased/Found From

History Behind Ticket

Ticket

NOTES

TICKET COLLECTION

Date of Ticket Event:

Details of Ticket:

Purchased/Found From

_____
_____
_____
_____
_____

History Behind Ticket

_____
_____
_____
_____
_____

Ticket

NOTES

_____
_____
_____
_____
_____

TICKET COLLECTION

Date of Ticket Event:

Details of Ticket:

Purchased/Found From

_____

_____

_____

_____

History Behind Ticket

_____

_____

_____

_____

_____

Ticket

NOTES

_____

_____

_____

_____

_____

TICKET COLLECTION

Date of Ticket Event:

Details of Ticket:

Purchased/Found From

_____
_____
_____
_____
_____

History Behind Ticket

_____
_____
_____
_____
_____

Ticket

NOTES

_____
_____
_____
_____
_____

TICKET COLLECTION

Date of Ticket Event: [   ]

Details of Ticket: [   ]

Purchased/Found From

_____
_____
_____
_____
_____

History Behind Ticket

_____
_____
_____
_____
_____

Ticket

NOTES

_____
_____
_____
_____

TICKET COLLECTION

Date of Ticket Event: [ ]

Details of Ticket: [ ]

Purchased/Found From

_____

_____

_____

_____

_____

History Behind Ticket

_____

_____

_____

_____

_____

Ticket

NOTES

_____

_____

_____

_____

_____

TICKET COLLECTION

Date of Ticket Event: [____]

Details of Ticket: [____]

Purchased/Found From

_____
_____
_____
_____
_____

History Behind Ticket

_____
_____
_____
_____
_____

Ticket

NOTES

_____
_____
_____
_____

TICKET COLLECTION Date of Ticket Event:

Details of Ticket:

Purchased/Found From

_____
_____
_____
_____
_____

History Behind Ticket

_____
_____
_____
_____
_____

Ticket

NOTES

_____
_____
_____
_____
_____

TICKET COLLECTION

Date of Ticket Event:

Details of Ticket:

Purchased/Found From

_____
_____
_____
_____
_____

History Behind Ticket

_____
_____
_____
_____
_____

Ticket

NOTES

_____
_____
_____
_____
_____

TICKET COLLECTION

Date of Ticket Event:

Details of Ticket:

Purchased/Found From

_____
_____
_____
_____

History Behind Ticket

_____
_____
_____
_____
_____

Ticket

NOTES

_____
_____
_____
_____
_____

TICKET COLLECTION Date of Ticket Event:

Details of Ticket:

Purchased/Found From

_____
_____
_____
_____
_____

History Behind Ticket

_____
_____
_____
_____
_____

Ticket

NOTES

_____
_____
_____
_____
_____

TICKET COLLECTION

Date of Ticket Event: [   ]

Details of Ticket: [   ]

Purchased/Found From

_____
_____
_____
_____
_____

History Behind Ticket

_____
_____
_____
_____
_____

Ticket

NOTES

_____
_____
_____
_____
_____

TICKET COLLECTION

Date of Ticket Event:

Details of Ticket:

Purchased/Found From

_____
_____
_____
_____
_____

History Behind Ticket

_____
_____
_____
_____
_____

Ticket

NOTES

_____
_____
_____
_____

TICKET COLLECTION

Date of Ticket Event:

Details of Ticket:

Purchased/Found From

_____

_____

_____

_____

_____

History Behind Ticket

_____

_____

_____

_____

_____

Ticket

NOTES

_____

_____

_____

_____

_____

TICKET COLLECTION Date of Ticket Event:

Details of Ticket:

Purchased/Found From

_____
_____
_____
_____
_____

History Behind Ticket

_____
_____
_____
_____
_____

Ticket

NOTES

_____
_____
_____
_____
_____

TICKET COLLECTION

Date of Ticket Event: [ ]

Details of Ticket: [ ]

Purchased/Found From

_____
_____
_____
_____
_____

History Behind Ticket

_____
_____
_____
_____
_____

Ticket

NOTES

_____
_____
_____
_____
_____

Printed in the USA
CPSIA information can be obtained
at www.ICGtesting.com
LVHW072305111223
766270LV00012B/377

9 781649 302533